GREAT MINDS
of Ancient Science
and Math

THE GREATEST MATHEMATICIAN

ARCHIMEDES AND HIS EUREKA! MOMENT

Titles in the *Great Minds of Ancient Science and Math* Series:

THE GREATEST MATHEMATICIAN:
ARCHIMEDES AND HIS EUREKA! MOMENT
ISBN-13: 978-0-7660-3408-2
ISBN-10:   0-7660-3408-9

THE GREAT THINKER:
ARISTOTLE AND THE FOUNDATIONS OF SCIENCE
ISBN-13: 978-0-7660-3121-0
ISBN-10:   0-7660-3121-7

THE FATHER OF THE ATOM:
DEMOCRITUS AND THE NATURE OF MATTER
ISBN-13: 978-0-7660-3410-5
ISBN-10:   0-7660-3410-0

MEASURING THE EARTH:
ERATOSTHENES AND HIS CELESTIAL GEOMETRY
ISBN-13: 978-0-7660-3120-3
ISBN-10:   0-7660-3120-9

THE FATHER OF GEOMETRY:
EUCLID AND HIS 3-D WORLD
ISBN-13: 978-0-7660-3409-9
ISBN-10:   0-7660-3409-7

THE FATHER OF ANATOMY:
GALEN AND HIS DISSECTIONS
ISBN-13: 978-0-7660-3380-1
ISBN-10:   0-7660-3380-5

THE GREATEST DOCTOR OF ANCIENT TIMES:
HIPPOCRATES AND HIS OATH
ISBN-13: 978-0-7660-3118-0
ISBN-10:   0-7660-3118-7

THE GREATEST MATHEMATICIAN

ARCHIMEDES AND HIS EUREKA! MOMENT

Paul Hightower

Enslow Pub
40 Industrial Road
Box 398
Berkeley Heights, NJ
USA

http://www.

Library of Congress Cataloging-in-Publication Data

Hightower, Paul (Paul W.)
    The greatest mathematician : Archimedes and his eureka! moment / Paul Hightower.
      p. cm. — (Great minds of ancient science and math)
    Summary: "A biography of ancient Greek mathematician Archimedes, who invented the compound pulley and other machines. His contributions to mathematics included devising the formulas for the surface and volume of a sphere"—Provided by publisher.
    Includes bibliographical references and index.
    ISBN-13: 978-0-7660-3408-2
    ISBN-10: 0-7660-3408-9
    1. Archimedes—Juvenile literature. 2. Mathematicians—Greece—Biography—Juvenile literature. I. Title.
    QA29.A7H54 2010
    510.92—dc22
    [B]

                        2008051818

Printed in the United States of America
052010 Lake Book Manufacturing, Inc., Melrose Park, IL
10 9 8 7 6 5 4 3 2

To Our Readers: We have done our best to make sure all Internet addresses in this book were active and appropriate when we went to press. However, the author and the publisher have no control over and assume no liability for the material available on those Internet sites or on other Web sites they may link to. Any comments or suggestions can be sent by e-mail to comments@enslow.com or to the address on the back cover.

✪ Enslow Publishers, Inc., is committed to printing our books on recycled paper. The paper in every book contains 10% to 30% post-consumer waste (PCW). The cover board on the outside of each book contains 100% PCW. Our goal is to do our part to help young people and the environment too!

Illustration Credits: Carsten Medom Madsen/Shutterstock, p. 61; Christie's Images/The Bridgeman Art Library, p. 82; David Wallace, MIT 2.009, <http://web.mit.edu/2.009/deathRay.html>, pp. 95, 96, 97; Enslow Publishers, Inc., pp. 11, 25, 31, 81; Galleria degli Uffizi, Florence, Italy/The Bridgeman Art Library, pp. 46, 65; The Granger Collection, New York, pp. 3, 9, 76; Heini Schneebeli/The Bridgeman Art Library, p. 35; Mary Evans Picture Library/Everett Collection, pp. 13, 66; Photos.com/© 2009 Jupiterimages Corporation, pp. 36, 51, 59, 86; Shutterstock, p. 100; Stephen J. Delisle, p. 39; Wikimedia Commons, p. 104; William Noel/The Walters Art Museum, pp. 88, 89; Yuriy Chertok/Shutterstock, p. 41.

Cover Illustration: The Granger Collection, New York.

CONTENTS

1

LIFE IN SYRACUSE

THE ROMAN SOLDIERS SAT PACKED INTO their warship. They had sailed from Rome as an invading army. They now neared their goal, the Greek city of Syracuse on the island of Sicily. It was less than a mile away, and they readied themselves for battle.

In the distance, the Romans could see the Greek soldiers preparing their defense. The Romans were worried because they had heard of the powerful war machines the Greeks had built. Their chief engineer, Archimedes, was always busy creating new devices to defend the city. The Romans had tried to conquer Syracuse for two years but failed every time.

They saw the Greeks moving a large structure around on the shore. It was as big as a house, and it gleamed as it reflected the light of the sun. It appeared to be a six-sided compound mirror, a larger mirror made up of smaller reflective panels. It turned on its base, and the Greeks pointed it straight at the Roman warship.

The Romans were blinded by the reflected light and had to shield their eyes. Minutes later, their ship began to smolder and smoke, and their sail burst into flames. The soldiers were forced to abandon their warship as the wood caught fire. They jumped into the sea, and their ship broke apart and sunk. Another Greek superweapon had defeated a Roman invasion.

Did this story actually happen? Did Archimedes invent a mirror that would burn invading warships from a distance? The simple truth is that we do not know for certain. There exist many sources and tales about Archimedes and his clever inventions. These stories began even during Archimedes' lifetime and have persisted for thousands of years. Separating

The Romans lose another battle against the Greeks. Archimedes is said to have built a weapon made up of giant mirrors that reflected sunlight onto the invading Roman fleet, destroying them by fire.

those stories that really happened from what has grown up around the ancient engineer is sometimes difficult.

The Western Greeks

The city of Syracuse was founded around 730 B.C., many centuries before Archimedes was born. It was an independent Greek colony on the island of Sicily in the Mediterranean Sea near modern-day Italy. Syracuse was one of the richest overseas cities of the ancient Greeks. It had deep harbors for heavy trade ships. It was a good stopping point for commercial ships from both Rome and Carthage.

Syracuse was in a unique location. It was part of what is known as *Magna Graecia*, an area of Greek colonies at the tip of Italy and the island of Sicily. As a Greek city-state, it was independent of the rest of Greece and had a democratic government. The people of Syracuse had defended the city against invaders from other parts of Sicily. Its wealth and independence made Syracuse the most powerful city in the western Mediterranean Sea.[1]

But Syracuse was caught between expanding empires. The Romans in Italy were growing in strength and influence. The Carthaginians on the northern coast of Africa were also a rising power. Syracuse was separated by sea from both Rome and Carthage, but it shared the island of Sicily with colonies loyal to Carthage. Rome and

Archimedes' birthplace, the Greek city of Syracuse in Sicily, and other important cities of his time.

Carthage would fight many times for power and influence, and both wanted to conquer Syracuse.

The cities of Sicily called upon the Greek general Pyrrhus to drive the occupying Roman and Carthaginian forces off the island. Pyrrhus did so in 278 B.C., and the newly freed cities of the island proclaimed him king of Sicily. Around 275 B.C., a Greek general named Hiero II, later to be named king, gained control of Syracuse. Hiero ruled for almost fifty years, and his reign was noted for peace and prosperity.[2]

Archimedes of Syracuse

Most of what we know about Archimedes comes from historians writing about him centuries later. Archimedes was born in Syracuse, although we do not know exactly when. The twelfth-century Byzantine writer Johannes Tzetzes claimed that Archimedes lived to be seventy-five years old.[3] We know that Archimedes died in Syracuse in 212 B.C. From these numbers, scholars estimate that Archimedes was born close to the year 287 B.C.

Archimedes, Greek mathematician and inventor, lived from about 287 to 212 B.C.

Very few records exist describing Archimedes and his family. Archimedes mentioned the name of his father, Pheidias, in the preface of one of his books. He also said that Pheidias was an astronomer. We do not know the name of Archimedes' mother, or if he had any brothers or sisters. We do not know if Archimedes ever married or had any children.

Many sources include descriptions of Archimedes' personality. Some historians try to portray him as an intense thinker, always concentrating on a new problem. Others write about how Archimedes was forgetful, or that he did not care about social or political issues. We do not know how accurate these images of Archimedes are. Almost all descriptions about Archimedes' personality come from other people writing about him centuries after his death.

Historians believe Archimedes may have been related to the royal family of Syracuse. He might have been close friends with Hiero and his son, Gelon. Under the reign of Hiero, Syracuse grew to be a great city of education and culture. Although not a wealthy man, Archimedes' family ties and friendship with the royal family allowed him time for his discoveries. And Hiero knew that keeping Archimedes close to him was good for Syracuse.

Major Sources for Archimedes

Today we have very little personal information about Archimedes, his life, or his personality. Most of his ideas and discoveries have been preserved in his writings. Some of his inventions were described by other ancient authors who lived around the same time. Some stories were written from oral histories retold centuries after Archimedes died.

However, many familiar tales about Archimedes are just legends. They come from various sources—stories that were told to present a dramatic picture of the man and his discoveries. Some stories might be based on a real idea but exaggerated to scare away invading armies. The story about the mirror weapon burning the warships was written by a Greek historian named Diodorus.[4] Diodorus lived about a century after Archimedes, and no proof exists that this invention was actually built. Some stories have been read and repeated so often that they are believed as fact. Only a very few of these events are actually true.

An important source for details about Archimedes' life is from an ancient Greek historian named Plutarch. Plutarch lived in the first century A.D., and he was well educated in local literature and history. He wrote a large book of biographies entitled *The Lives of the Noble Grecians and Romans,* often known as Plutarch's *Lives.* This book is one of our major sources of ancient Greek and Roman history.

One of the Romans that Plutarch wrote about was Marcus Claudius Marcellus. Marcellus was an important general and consul, a chief magistrate, who led the attack on Syracuse. The Greeks held off Marcellus and his army for two years armed with Archimedes' inventions. Marcellus and his soldiers fought against new

Greek weapons credited to Archimedes. Because of this, a few details of Archimedes' life are included in Plutarch's biography of Marcellus.

Plutarch wrote about Archimedes that "he used to trace geometrical figures in the ashes of the fire, and diagrams in the oil on his body, being in a state of entire preoccupation, and . . . divine possession with his love and delight in science."[5] Archimedes seemed to have had a pure devotion to his mathematics, thinking about it constantly. However, we do not know if this is a true description of Archimedes' character, as Plutarch lived centuries after Archimedes died.

Other Historical Sources

Another ancient writer who is a source of information about Archimedes' life is Marcus Tullius Cicero. Cicero was a Roman statesman and orator who lived in the first century B.C. He studied a great deal of Greek philosophy and wrote about it for the Romans. Cicero wrote many books and left behind a great number of letters. He also claimed to have discovered the abandoned tomb of Archimedes while in Syracuse.

Most of Archimedes' scientific and mathematical ideas come from books he wrote himself. The originals of these works are long lost, but they were copied over and over. Archimedes would often address other mathematicians in the prefaces of these books. We can gather small details about Archimedes' life and his relationships from these personal notes to his friends and colleagues.

Other cultures such as the Romans and the Arabs used Archimedes' writings as textbooks. These manuscripts were copied and translated for thousands of years, even well into the Renaissance. Some copies, such as the Archimedes Palimpsest, were not analyzed until the twentieth century. A new work written by Archimedes was discovered within this palimpsest.[6] Work on this palimpsest is very recent, and we are still learning new facts about Archimedes even today.

2
ARCHIMEDES AS MATHEMATICIAN

ARCHIMEDES WAS AGAIN BUSY WORKING on a new problem. He was tracing figures in the sand with a stick, trying to find a solution. His meal sat untouched on a nearby table. Hours had passed since the meal was brought to him, but Archimedes did not notice. His only focus was on the problem at hand, and the rest of the world was ignored.

Likewise, his appearance was that of a poor man. Archimedes wore a tunic that was dirty and neglected. The edges had started to tear, and parts of the cloth were so thin you could see through them. His hair and beard were also messy. Archimedes did not care about his appearance or even to bathe himself. His only focus was on the mathematics problem in front of him.

Is this description of the absentminded mathematician true? Did Archimedes concentrate on his work so much that he neglected personal and social habits? Many authors and historians have repeated this profile of Archimedes' behavior. However, there are no firsthand written accounts of his personality or of any of these traits. Many of these stories come from later writers themselves, not from actual accounts of Archimedes' life.

Some authors such as Plutarch describe Archimedes as an idealistic mathematician. Plutarch wrote that Archimedes considered "sordid and ignoble the whole trade of engineering." He believed Archimedes preferred the pure and perfect study of mathematics and that practical applications were beneath him. But some historians do not believe Archimedes felt this way.[1] Some believe descriptions such as this are from Plutarch and his interpretation rather than Archimedes' true nature. Archimedes left behind works of mathematical theory as well as scientific and engineering studies.

Study in Alexandria

Archimedes spent most of his life in Syracuse. However, he did travel to Alexandria in Egypt as a young man to study mathematics. At this time, Alexandria was the largest city in the world and a center for education. It also had a deep harbor, and it had grown into a major trade city. Alexandria attracted the best scholars, artists, and scientists from around the world.

While studying in Alexandria, Archimedes met two men who would be his good friends for the rest of his life. One was named Conon and the other was named Eratosthenes, both gifted mathematicians. Conon was an astronomer in the court of Ptolemy III, the ruler of Alexandria. Eratosthenes was a tutor to Ptolemy's son and the chief librarian at the great library at Alexandria. Eratosthenes is best remembered for calculating a very accurate value for the circumference of Earth.[2]

Conon was the mathematician who developed what is now known as the Archimedes spiral. This figure is a very regular and perfect spiral produced by moving at a constant radial speed and constant angular velocity. Imagine a fly walking along a straight line drawn outward from the center of a circle, except the circle is spinning. The actual path of the fly traces out an Archimedes spiral.

Archimedes wrote about the properties of this spiral in his book *On Spirals*. He calculated the area of the spiral after each complete revolution. After the second revolution, "the area added by the spiral in the third revolution will be double of that added in the second, . . . and generally the areas added in the later revolutions will be multiples of that added in the second revolution."[3] This geometric series has many uses for other geometrical constructions and solutions. The spiral design also has a few engineering applications as well.

Archimedes exchanged letters with both Conon and Eratosthenes for years after leaving Alexandria. Some of these letters were included as a preface to Archimedes' books. Even after Conon died years later, Archimedes continued to write to one of Conon's students, named Dositheus.[4] Most of what we know about this mathematician Dositheus comes from these letters of Archimedes.

The Method of Exhaustion

One of the most important works of Archimedes is his calculation of an approximate value of pi (π). Pi is defined as the ratio of the circumference of a circle to its diameter. Pi is an irrational number, meaning that it has a decimal portion that never ends and never repeats. It is used in many mathematics problems involving circles and curves. Calculating an accurate value of pi has been a goal of mathematicians since ancient times.

Calculating the perimeter of a polygon is simple, and its value is exact. However, calculating the circumference of a circle requires knowing the value of pi, and the circumference is difficult to measure accurately. Archimedes approached this problem by drawing two polygons, one outside and one inside a circle. The perimeters of these two polygons provided an upper and lower limit for the circumference of the circle between them.

By increasing the number of sides on each polygon, the perimeters of the polygons become closer and closer to the circumference of the circle. Think of shortening the edges of a polygon until they are so small that they feel smooth, like a perfectly round circle. Archimedes began with hexagons (six sides) and eventually used polygons of ninety-six sides each to calculate these perimeters. He estimated the value of pi was between $3^{10}/_{71}$ and $3^1/_7$, the most accurate value at that time.[5]

But more important than his calculated value of pi was the process Archimedes used. This method of increasing the number of sides on a polygon to approximate the curve of a circle is an example of the method of exhaustion. This method was first demonstrated by the Greek mathematician Eudoxus, who lived about a century before Archimedes. Archimedes describes this method of exhaustion in his book *Measurement of the Circle*.

The area of the polygon can be calculated exactly, but it will never exactly equal the area of the circle. The idea of the method of exhaustion

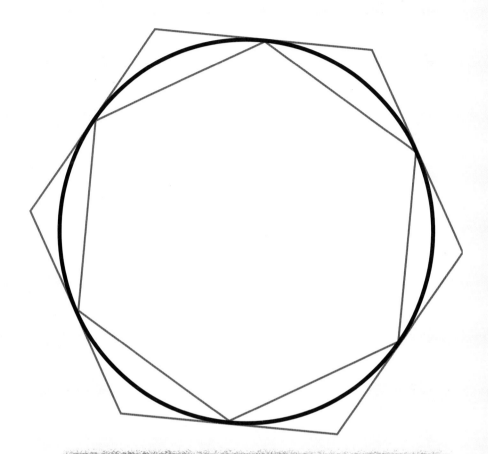

Archimedes used the method of exhaustion to calculate an approximate value of pi. He figured out the perimeters of two polygons, one outside and one inside a circle. The circumference of the circle would be a value between the two perimeters. The greater the number of sides on each polygon, the closer the polygons' perimeters would be to the circle's circumference, and therefore, the more accurate the approximation of pi would be.

is to construct a polygon with enough sides so its area is "arbitrarily close" to that area bounded by a curve. If the difference between the two areas is small enough, then the area of the polygon provides a good approximate value for the area of a circle.

"Thus, by continuing the process," Archimedes wrote, "we shall ultimately arrive at a circumscribed polygon such that the spaces intercepted between it and the circle are together less than the excess . . . over the area of the circle."[6] By making the number of sides greater, the length of these included sides becomes smaller. Thus, the difference between the area of the polygon and that bounded by the curve is "exhausted."

Archimedes used this method of exhaustion in many of his books and for many different shapes. This method of exhaustion used by Archimedes was a forerunner to a modern mathematical approach called calculus. Calculus would not be developed formally until the seventeenth century by Isaac Newton and Gottfried Leibniz. Today, calculus is fundamental to almost all areas of modern science and engineering.

The Sand-Reckoner

Ancient Greek mathematicians did not use the same numerals we use today. Today's symbols (the digits 1 through 9 and zero) are called Arabic numerals, and they were not developed until about A.D. 500. Both the Greeks and the Romans used letters from their alphabets to denote numbers. The Greek letter alpha (α) would equal 1, the letter beta (β) would equal 2, and so on. Also, the Greeks had no letter to denote zero.

For larger numbers, this system becomes very complicated. Different letters were used for tens (10, 20, 30 . . . 90) and for hundreds (100, 200, 300 . . . 900). Numbers were formed by adding the letter values, so the number "327" would be written with three Greek letters as "300+ 20+7." Special characters were also used for larger numbers above 1,000.

Archimedes became interested in a theoretical mathematics puzzle. He wanted to calculate the number of grains of sand that would fill the whole universe. Archimedes calculated the size of a grain of sand and then estimated the size of the universe (the earth, sun, and stars) known at that time. He wrote about his calculations in a book called *The Sand-Reckoner*. This book is also sometimes called by its title in Greek, *Psammites,* or by its title in Latin, *Arenarius*.

For the size of the known universe, Archimedes relied on the work of an earlier Greek astronomer Aristarchus. Although his actual size estimation was not correct, Aristarchus was the first to put the sun at the center of the universe with the earth and other planets orbiting it. This type of arrangement is known as the heliocentric model. This model of the solar system would be rediscovered by Nicolaus Copernicus almost two thousand years later.

Archimedes writes that Aristarchus claimed "the fixed stars and the sun remain unmoved, that the earth revolves about the sun in the circumference of a circle, the sun lying in the middle of the orbit."[7] The stars were believed to lie on the surface of a distant cosmic sphere. The sun, the moon, and all the planets were included within this celestial sphere. This was the model of the universe that Archimedes used.

Very Large Numbers

Using principles of geometry, Archimedes calculated the size of the known universe. He also calculated the size of an average grain of sand, which he estimated as no larger than a poppy seed. Archimedes then concluded that the number of grains of sand required would be 10^{63}. This value is written as the numeral 1 followed by sixty-three zeros. This is an extremely large number, and writing out this entire value in full is awkward.

What is important about *The Sand-Reckoner* is not the value that Archimedes calculated but some of the methods he developed to use very large numbers. The Greeks used the letter *M*, called a myriad, for the number 10,000. The number 100,000,000 was called a myriad-

myriad, and this was the largest number the ancient Greeks used. Numbers larger than a myriad-myriad were just too complicated to write with their number system.

Archimedes developed a system to simplify and expand the notation for very large numbers. He used a system of octads—groups of eight powers of ten, such as 10^0, 10^1, 10^2 . . . 10^7—that add together to build up very large numbers like 10^{63}. Archimedes was no longer limited by the upper bound of the myriad-myriad. His number system could count up to a number that had eighty thousand million million digits.[8]

Archimedes enjoyed mathematical puzzles, and he wrote about a game called the *Stomachion*. This was a puzzle of fourteen differently shaped pieces that fit together to form a square. These pieces could be arranged in different combinations to make the same square. Archimedes tried to calculate how many different solutions existed for this puzzle. (Modern mathematicians have shown there are 17,152 unique solutions to this problem.)[9]

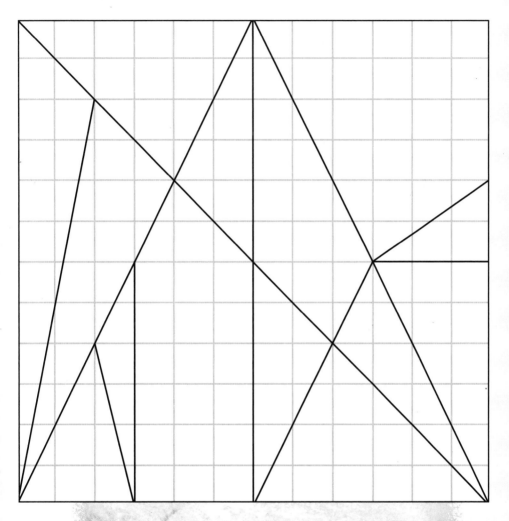

A stomachion is made up of fourteen different geometric pieces that can be arranged more than seventeen thousand different ways to form the same square.

Archimedes also studied and wrote about many problems in geometry. He studied the properties of circles, cylinders, cones, and spheres. He wrote about problems like these in his books *On the Sphere and Cylinder* and *On Conoids and Spheroids*. These books deal with the properties of all sorts of three-dimensional shapes. Much of Archimedes' work would form the basis for various fields of mathematics more than a thousand years later.

HIERO'S GOLD CROWN

ARCHIMEDES WAS CONSTANTLY THINKING about his experiments and research. Even in the bath, his mind would still concentrate on finding a solution. It did not matter whether his problem was mathematical theory or some engineering challenge asked of him by the king. Archimedes was more concerned with solutions than soap and water.

But today, it was the water that provided a solution. Archimedes noticed that when he sat down in his bath, the water level would rise. When he stood up, the water level would fall. Everyone sees this same event every time they sit in a bath or a small pool of water. But this time, Archimedes saw more than just the water level rising and falling. He saw the solution to his problem.

Archimedes had been working on this problem for weeks. He was so excited to find a solution that he immediately jumped up out of his bath. He ran dripping wet out of the house and through the streets of Syracuse, shouting about his success. Archimedes was so happy to find the new solution, he did not even realize he was naked.

This story is perhaps the most famous tale associated with Archimedes. But did he really run out of his bath and through the streets naked? Was Archimedes so excited by his solution that he forgot about everything else, including his modesty? Again, we cannot know if this story is true. It comes from a Roman architect and engineer named Vitruvius who lived in the first century B.C., about two hundred years after Archimedes.[1]

"Eureka!"

The problem put before Archimedes came from the King, Hiero. The king wanted a crown made

The gold crown in question probably resembled this gold wreath of oak leaves and acorns from the fourth century B.C.

of pure gold. He contracted with a goldsmith and gave him details and an exact amount of gold to use. After a few days, the goldsmith returned with a finished crown. But the gossip that arose was that the goldsmith had substituted silver for some of the gold. He had used only part of the gold in the crown and kept the rest for himself.

How could Hiero know if his crown was pure gold? The only way to test the metal was to destroy the crown. The task the king gave to Archimedes was to determine the purity of the gold in his crown without damaging it. What

Legend has it that Archimedes discovered the principle of displacement while settling into his bath.

Archimedes noticed in his bath was that the water level rose when he sat down. In other words, his body displaced a certain volume of water. In his bath, Archimedes discovered the principle of displacement.

Displacement literally means "pushed aside," in this case the volume of water that is pushed out of the way by another object. This principle of displacement was the important key in Archimedes' discovery. Because water has no shape of its own, the shape of the object displacing the water did not matter. So excited was Archimedes by this discovery that he ran from his bath shouting in Greek, *"Heureka! Heureka!"* which means "I have found it!" (Common English spells the word without the "H"—"Eureka!")

Hiero's Crown

Archimedes immediately set up a test for his new theory. As told by Vitruvius, Archimedes made two masses both equal in weight to the crown. One mass was of pure gold and one was of pure silver. He filled a vessel right to the brim and dropped in the silver mass. A certain amount of water spilled out, and this overflow volume corresponded to a certain displacement. Archimedes refilled the vessel to the brim and repeated the trial with the gold mass. Again, a certain amount of water spilled out.

When Archimedes compared the volume of overflow water from the gold mass, he found it was less than that of the silver mass. Gold is a much heavier metal than silver, meaning that gold has a greater density than silver. Density is the ratio of the mass of a substance per unit volume. Even though the weights of these two masses were the same, their densities were different. This method was how Archimedes could tell the difference between the two metals.

Archimedes then refilled the vessel to the brim and dropped in the gold crown. A certain amount of water spilled out, and he collected and measured the volume of the spilled water. The volume of water displaced by the crown did not equal the volume of water displaced by a

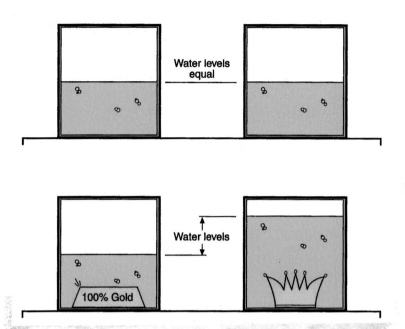

This diagram illustrates the principle of displacement Archimedes used to determine the purity of the king's gold crown. The king's crown pushed aside more water than a bar of pure gold with the same weight. The volume of the crown was greater than the volume of the block of gold. The crown's density was not equal to the density of the gold bar, therefore, the crown was not made of pure gold.

mass of pure gold of the same weight. The density of the crown did not match the density of pure gold. Archimedes determined that the metal used in the crown was not all gold but a mix of gold and silver.[2]

The Archimedes Principle

Archimedes wrote about his discoveries with water in a book called *On Floating Bodies*. This book established the field of hydrostatics, the study of forces and equilibrium in fluids. Archimedes outlined two basic principles of hydrostatics in this book:

1. Any solid lighter than a fluid will be so far immersed that the weight of the solid will be equal to the weight of the fluid displaced.

2. Any solid heavier than a fluid will descend to the bottom, and, when weighed in the fluid, the solid will be lighter than its true weight by the weight of the fluid displaced.[3]

These two statements introduce the concept of buoyancy. Buoyancy is the upward force of the surrounding water on a submerged object. Objects with a density less than water, such as wood or paper, float on top because their buoyancy is greater than their weight. Objects with a density greater than water sink because their weight is greater than their buoyancy. If an

The Archimedes' principle still guides modern naval architecture. This cruise ship floats because the weight of the water displaced by its hull is equal to the weight of the entire ship and everything inside it.

object's buoyancy is equal to its weight, the object will neither sink nor float.

This idea of buoyancy leads to what is called the Archimedes principle. This law states that the buoyant force of an object in water equals the weight of the water displaced by the object. Objects weigh less in water than in air because of their buoyancy. The magnitude of the buoyant force can be calculated by the water the object displaces.[4]

This principle is fundamental to almost any area of science or engineering that deals with water, water pressure, or the sea. It is used in all areas of naval and underwater research and in any field involving the design of ships or ocean vessels. Many commercial ships are rated by their displacement, which is related to how much cargo they can carry. Because air can be considered a fluid, The Archimedes principle can also be used with balloons and airships.

Buoyancy at Work

A second method of testing the purity of Hiero's crown is related by an anonymous Latin text from around A.D. 500. Vitruvius tells of a method that used the principle of displacement. This second source describes Archimedes using a method of buoyancy. Which method Archimedes really used, or if he used a different method, is not known for certain.

The crown and a mass of pure gold of the same weight were hung on a balance scale. Because their weights are equal in air, the scale was balanced. If either the crown or the gold mass were submerged in water, they would both have buoyant forces acting on them. These buoyant forces are related to the relative densities of each mass. The buoyant forces acting on these masses cause them to weigh less in water than in air.

Archimedes then placed the trays of the balance scale in a large vessel of water. If the densities of the crown and the gold mass were equal, the scale would remain in balance. But if the densities were not equal, the buoyancy of one mass would be greater than the buoyancy of the other. With different buoyant forces on the two objects, the scale would not stay balanced. If the crown was not pure gold, its density would be less and its buoyancy would be greater than pure gold.[5]

Archimedes also wrote about the buoyancy and stability of various objects in water. Many of these methods are related to the ability of very heavy ships to float without sinking. Some problems even detail the conditions under which a ship may be too tall and might tip over while at sea. The mathematical proofs that Archimedes provided in *On Floating Bodies* have guided the science of shipbuilding for more than a thousand years.

4

ON THE EQUILIBRIUM OF PLANES

ARCHIMEDES SPENT MUCH OF HIS WORK studying the lever, the pulley, and the screw. These are a few of the basic machines known to physics and called simple machines. Archimedes tried to explain to King Hiero about the principles he discovered. Using these tools, Archimedes believed that any object could be moved, no matter how heavy.

Hiero was skeptical and demanded a demonstration. He had a cargo ship that was still in its dock. Archimedes studied the problem and devised a series of levers, ropes, and pulleys to tow the ship. While he prepared the demonstration, the ship was filled with passengers and a full load of freight. Archimedes took hold of the

This painting depicts Archimedes pulling a ship ashore using a machine known as an endless screw.

last of the ropes and pulled. Through a series of simple machines, Archimedes alone moved the ship out of the dock and into the open water![1]

But Archimedes did much more than just build amazing tools. He used geometry and simple logic to explain how these tools worked. He not only used the lever but he wrote an analysis about what made the lever work. He provided a mathematical way to think about physics, which is different than just demonstrating an experiment. Archimedes provided a basis for the concept of mathematical and theoretical physics.

Statics and Mechanics

One of the major contributions of Archimedes to science was his study of mechanics. Mechanics is a basic field of physics that is concerned with forces acting on an object. Mechanics can be broken down into two other areas: statics and kinetics. Statics is the study of all the forces acting on an object in equilibrium, or on a body that is standing still. While you sit in your chair, you still have various forces acting on you, such as gravity and the force of the chair pushing upward.

Kinetics is the study of forces acting on an object in motion. When you throw a ball, that ball moves under the force you gave it to move forward. It also has other forces acting against its movement, such as wind resistance and gravity. Kinetics can be very complex because the forces can change as the object moves. By comparison, statics is simpler because it deals with forces in equilibrium.

47

Archimedes preferred studying problems of statics instead of kinetics. He found that the conditions of equilibrium could be well represented by mathematical descriptions, particularly geometry. The physical laws that describe the forces on a moving body seemed complex and unclear to Archimedes. Even today, kinetics is a more difficult science than statics because of all the forces involved.

Archimedes wrote about problems of statics in his book called *On the Equilibrium of Planes*. This book was not the first written about this subject. About a century earlier, the great philosopher Aristotle wrote a similar book called simply *Physics*. Archimedes' book came in two volumes, whereas Aristotle's book filled eight volumes. But this is not the only difference between the two texts.

Aristotle relied more on kinetics to prove his ideas. For the lever, his description of its properties involved calculating how each arm traced out a circular path as it moved. Aristotle deduced the physical law for the lever from its relative motion. However, Archimedes relied on statics and geometry to describe the lever in equilibrium. Archimedes was able to provide a logical mathematical proof for the principles of the lever from basic postulates.[2]

Archimedes always demanded proof for his conclusions. Physically demonstrating that a principle was correct was not enough. He always wanted to reduce the problem to one of mathematics, and then prove the concept correct mathematically. Archimedes would not consider a concept "proven" until it had been proven with mathematics. This manner of abstract proof for physical principles was a big step forward for theoretical physics.

The Lever

The lever is one of the six simple machines of physics. These simple machines are the lever, the wheel, the pulley, the inclined plane, the screw, and the wedge. From these simple machines, all other machines can be constructed. What these simple machines provide is something called mechanical advantage. Mechanical advantage means that the machine multiplies the force put into it to produce a much larger force.

Archimedes worked out the lever's mathematical principles from basic postulates. He demonstrated mathematically that the lever provides a mechanical advantage. He also found a way to calculate that advantage. Archimedes reduced the problem to one of simple geometry. He imagined the lever as a weightless line with two masses, one on either side of the fulcrum. He began with the principle that masses of equal weight at equal distances from the fulcrum are in equilibrium.

If you replace a mass with one that weighs twice as much, you must move it half the distance to the fulcrum to maintain equilibrium. This relationship between the mass and the distance to the fulcrum is generalized in the law of the lever.[3] The law of the lever in equilibrium can be stated in an equation as

$$m_1 d_1 = m_2 d_2$$

In this equation, m_1 and m_2 represent the masses on each side of the fulcrum. The values of d_1 and d_2 are the distances of each mass from the fulcrum, respectively.

This mathematical equation is a very powerful physical law. Notice that there are no restrictions on either the mass or the distance. In theory, an object of any weight can be moved if the distance to the fulcrum is great enough. Archimedes stated this as "given the force, any

An image of Archimedes moving the earth with a lever.

given weight might be moved, even . . . if there were another earth." In the fourth century A.D., the Greek mathematician Pappus expressed this statement in more familiar words: "Give me a firm spot on which to stand and I will move the Earth."[4]

Centers of Gravity

Archimedes wrote about the lever in his two-volume book, *On the Equilibrium of Planes*. Also found in these volumes is the concept of the center of gravity of an object. The center of gravity is the point on an object at which the mass can be balanced, as if the object had no dimensions or shape. In a one-dimensional model, the center of gravity of a lever at equilibrium is at its fulcrum.

Archimedes wrote about the centers of gravity of many different geometrical shapes. He calculated the centers of gravity for triangles, trapezoids, and segments of a parabola. These centers of gravity were found using much the same method that Archimedes used for the lever.

His geometry could establish the center of gravity of an object without resorting to an experiment to prove it.[5]

The concept of the center of gravity is important to the field of mechanics. One problem that arises when working with real-world experiments is that objects have structure. That is, objects have a shape, are composed of different materials, and have an unequal distribution of weight. By considering the center of gravity, we can deal with that object as a single point instead of an irregular, complicated mass. This simplification makes the mathematics easier, no matter if the object is a baseball or an airplane or a planet orbiting the sun.

The center of gravity is also important to the science of shipbuilding. Archimedes studied the centers of gravity and various other properties of parabolas in his book, *Quadrature of the Parabola*. These parabolas can be used to approximate the shape of a ship's hull in the water. If the center of gravity of a ship is too high, it will become unstable. An unstable ship will tip over and sink at sea.

The Method

Archimedes wrote another book called *The Method of Mechanical Theorems,* or known as *The Method* for short. This book is also filled with mathematical proofs for problems of mechanics. Archimedes describes the solution to a problem mechanically and then proves the same problem mathematically. He did not accept that demonstrating a solution by experiment is the same as a formal proof of the physical principle at work.

Other books by Archimedes only included the final proof of the problem at hand. *The Method* is important because it describes the process by which Archimedes found his solutions.[6] He created a thought experiment with two masses on a lever, then he "balanced" them using their weights and distances to the center. Archimedes used geometry to prove the law of the lever instead of a physics experiment.

Some later writers criticized Archimedes for not fully explaining some of his solutions. These writers never knew about this manuscript, as *The*

Method was only recently discovered. It was found in an old prayer book, with the original text hiding beneath the later content. *The Method* provides a look inside the thoughts of Archimedes. It demonstrates his reasoning as he developed proofs for some of his mathematical problems.

OTHER INVENTIONS

JUST AS HE COULD OBSESS OVER MATH-ematical problems, Archimedes also liked to tinker with machines. He would invent instruments to assist in his studies or to demonstrate a principle of mechanics. Sometimes he would invent a device to solve a problem, such as pumping water to irrigate crops. King Hiero used Archimedes' talent to design weapons to defend Syracuse against invasion.

Astronomical Inventions

Archimedes studied astronomy and associated with astronomers while in Alexandria. His friends Conon and Eratosthenes were both accomplished astronomers. We can assume that

Archimedes was introduced to astronomy by his father, Pheidias, who was also an astronomer. The mathematics that Archimedes studied helped him solve astronomical problems.

One of Archimedes' inventions was a sort of astronomical tool used for observations of our night sky. The sun, moon, and planets were mounted on tracks and revolved around a center ball representing the earth. The movement was mechanical, like the inside of a clock, and controlled by turning a wheel or dial.[1] Today we call this device a planetarium, as it represents the sky as viewed from the earth.

Historians believe that Archimedes built at least two of these planetarium devices. Both were taken to Rome after Syracuse was conquered. The Roman writer Cicero claimed to examine one of these instruments that was owned by the family of Marcellus. Archimedes allegedly wrote about the mathematics and construction of these planetarium tools in his book *On Sphere-Making*. However, this book has never been found.

City and Industrial Inventions

Archimedes is credited with inventing a type of water pump based on what is called an Archimedean screw. Historians believe Archimedes might have invented this device while studying in Alexandria. In Egypt, the only source of water for irrigating crops was the Nile River. Archimedes might have been asked to provide a solution for this problem.

An Archimedean screw is a long piece of metal twisted around a center axis and mounted within a tight-fitting cylinder. At the end of the axis is a handle for the operator to turn. With one end submerged in water at an angle, turning the handle causes the screw to rotate. The water inside the screw moves up, like a moving staircase. When it reaches the top, the water spills out. The Archimedean screw can be as long as necessary, making this tool ideal for pumping water to a higher level.

Some Arabic translations refer to a lost book Archimedes wrote about water clocks. Water-powered clocks were built and used centuries

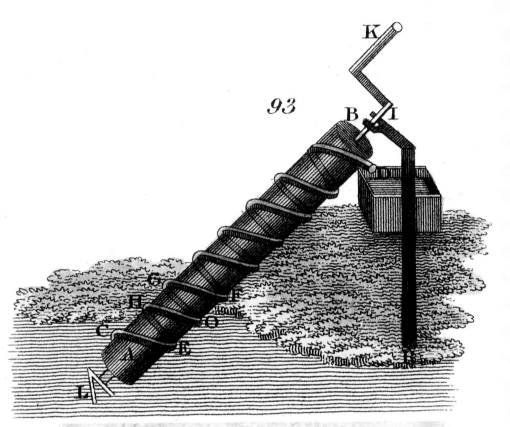

This diagram shows a water pump based on an Archimedean screw.

before Archimedes. However, the clock that Archimedes built was accurate to within two minutes each day. These sources are translations, and the translator may have credited Archimedes only because he knew the reputation of this mathematician. Because no clear proof exists, historians debate whether this clock was invented by Archimedes or by another Greek scientist.[2]

Many other devices are credited to Archimedes, but proof for these inventions has not been absolutely established. Archimedes built an instrument to measure the diameter of the sun. He invented an odometer, a device for measuring how far a cart has traveled. He developed various types of winches and siphons and a few tools operated by wind or steam power. Historians are not sure if Archimedes invented these devices or if he built his own improved versions of other scientists' inventions. He built his own scientific instruments, so it is possible that he constructed these machines.

Naval Machines

The most important work of Archimedes to naval engineering was with compound pulleys. A compound pulley is just many pulleys connected together so that their mechanical advantage is greater than that of an individual pulley. By using a system of ropes and compound pulleys, one person can lift or pull objects much heavier than they could do otherwise.

Archimedes is believed to have developed a compound pulley known as a "block and tackle." This block and tackle system is made up of two pulleys with a rope threaded between them, often several times. This tool was important to ancient sailors, as it is to modern sailors. The

A block and tackle system.

block and tackle allows individual sailors to move heavy sails and nets while their ships are far from land.

Archimedes also designed a system to launch the largest ship in all of the ancient world. It was called the *Syrakosia* and could carry a cargo load of two thousand tons. Plutarch reports that Archimedes, "sitting himself the while far off, with no great endeavor, but only holding the head of a pulley in his hand and drawing the cords by degree, he drew the ship in a straight line, as smoothly and evenly as if she had been in the sea."[3]

The *Syrakosia* was likely built by King Hiero for political purposes, not commerce. It was so large that it was useless for trade. No harbors other than Syracuse and Alexandria were deep enough to receive it. Hiero sent it to Alexandria and gave it as a gift to Ptolemy, and then it never sailed again. Another ship of this size would not be built until the nineteenth century.[4]

Some historians also speculate about whether Archimedes adapted his screw to launch other ships. Using much larger versions, two opposite-thread screws would be placed on either side of a ship constructed in a dry dock. With the ship resting on the screws, each screw was turned in opposite directions. The ship would then ride the thread of the screws forward until the ship reached the water.

Military Inventions

To Archimedes, his discoveries were a simple science lesson, a demonstration of a physical principle. But King Hiero saw the practical uses of these tools. Hiero used Archimedes' knowledge and enthusiasm for solving problems to build up Syracuse's defenses. Archimedes designed all types of clever instruments and weapons that would prove useful against an invading enemy.

Many of Archimedes' inventions were types of catapults. These were machines used to hurl either heavy stones or sharpened objects at a distant enemy. If the enemy was close enough, other inventions would simply swing an arm out over the city wall and drop a large weight, crushing the attackers. Some of these weights were as heavy as five hundred pounds.

Researchers still debate whether Archimedes successfully developed another weapon—a large mirror to ignite ships at sea. With his study of optics and reflection, Archimedes might have invented a smaller mirror. This mirror would focus the light of the sun to start a small fire. The story of the large-mirrored superweapon comes from the Roman writer Lucius in the second century A.D.[5] This story may have been based on a smaller real experiment, if not a functional full-sized weapon.

One of the devices that Archimedes developed was used to overturn entire ships. It resembled a modern-day crane with a long boom that would swing out over the water. It had a claw that would grab one end of a ship and lift that end straight up out of the water. When the ship was high enough, the device would release and the ship would fall and overturn in the harbor. As Marcellus commented about this device,

This illustration reconstructs the crane-like device with the claw Archimedes invented to overturn the Roman ships.

"Archimedes uses my ships to ladle seawater into his wine cups."[6]

Archimedes may have also invented a powerful steam-powered cannon. The design of this cannon is shown in the notebooks of the Italian Renaissance artist and scientist, Leonardo da Vinci. Water would be forced into a heated metal cannon behind a cannonball. The water

A soldier fires off a steam-powered cannon, possibly invented by Archimedes.

would instantly turn to steam, and the pressure would force the cannonball out. Leonardo lived more than 1,600 years after Archimedes, but he credits Archimedes with this invention in his *Notebooks*.

6

THE SACK OF SYRACUSE

THE EMERGING EMPIRES OF ROME AND Carthage would fight a series of three wars during the third and second centuries B.C. These wars were fought for control of the lands of the western Mediterranean Sea. Rome eventually defeated Carthage and became the major empire that we read about in history books. These conflicts were called the Punic Wars because the Latin name for the Carthaginians was *Punici,* or descendants of the Phoenicians.

The First Punic War (264–241 B.C.) was fought just a few years after Archimedes was born. There was no clear winner between Rome and Carthage in the First Punic War. Because of its location, the city of Syracuse was spared much of this conflict. However, Rome gained territory on the island of Sicily, which led to Syracuse's involvement in the Second Punic War.

The Third and last Punic War (149–146 B.C.) was fought more than sixty years after Archimedes died. By that time, Rome had grown into a powerful Mediterranean empire. This war was not evenly matched, and Rome easily destroyed what remained of Carthage and its empire. But it was the Second Punic War that involved Archimedes and his inventions.

The Second Punic War

The Second Punic War (218–201 B.C.) began much as the First Punic War did. Conflicts arose continuously between Rome and Carthage over influence and territory. Peace treaties were signed but rarely lasted, as both empires continued to grow and expand. Carthage had recently occupied what is today Spain, and now it had a foothold in Europe. The Carthaginian general Hannibal was raising an army in Europe to attack Rome.

Initially, Syracuse was left out of the Second Punic War. King Hiero was a faithful ally to Rome, and he supported the war effort. He sent thousands of soldiers and millions of bushels of grain to the Roman governor of Sicily.[1] But Hiero was a very old man, and he died in 215 B.C. of natural causes. His son Gelon had died the previous year, so King Hiero was succeeded by his grandson, Hieronymus.

Hieronymus was only about fifteen years old and poorly prepared to rule the city. He immediately made an alliance with Hannibal to force the Romans off the island of Sicily. His countrymen hated him, as now he made an enemy of Rome. Even Carthage considered Hieronymus untrustworthy and unpredictable. By the end of the year, a conspiracy was formed and Hieronymus was assassinated. The remaining members of Hiero's family were also brutally murdered, even the women and children.

Afterward, Syracuse sought to repair political relations with Rome and renew its alliance. But Carthaginian agents named Hippocrates and

Epicydes were already at work to influence the city. These two men lived in Syracuse for some time, and were elected to the Board of Generals. They used propaganda and lies to convince the people of Syracuse that Rome was a threat, and that Carthage was their ally.[2]

However, the damage was already done, and Rome was now an enemy. The task of taking control of the island of Sicily was given to the Roman general Marcus Claudius Marcellus. Marcellus was an accomplished soldier and leader, having fought Hannibal in Europe. In 214 B.C., his goals were now set on conquering Syracuse for Rome.

A City Under Siege

Initially, Marcellus did not expect much resistance from Syracuse. Syracuse was not known as a major military force. It was protected only by large, strong walls surrounding the city. However, the old king, Hiero, used Archimedes' talents to build great defenses for his city. The city of Syracuse held back the assault of the

Romans from both land and sea for more than two years.

The Roman ships came under such a fierce assault by missiles and stones that the navy was driven back. Marcellus was unsure of the Greeks' strength, so he ordered a retreat to a safe distance. Thinking that Syracuse possessed only long-range weapons, Marcellus ordered a night attack by land. He thought that the Roman soldiers could gain an advantage by approaching behind the range of the Greek catapults.

But Marcellus was mistaken. The Roman soldiers were again attacked with the same fury as before. Archimedes designed a series of similar weapons but of different sizes. When the enemy came closer, the Greeks would switch to shorter-range weapons. No matter how near or far the enemy was the Greek weapons would always reach them. There was no safe distance for the Roman troops.

The Romans were repeatedly repelled, and the defenses protected Syracuse. Warships were lifted out of the water with strange claws, and heavy stones hurled through the air would sink other ships. Marcellus was frustrated and confused with his lack of success. At the same time, he was also impressed with the genius of Archimedes and his inventions. "Must we give up fighting with this geometrical Briareus," Marcellus said, "who plays pitch-and-toss with our ships, and, with the multitude of darts which he showers at a single moment upon us, really outdoes the hundred-handed giants of mythology?"[3]

Archimedes' inventions were very successful at defending his city. Eventually, the sight of any loose rope or small piece of wood on the walls of Syracuse would strike fear in the Romans. They could not know the imagination of Archimedes. They were afraid of some new and astonishing device that would kill them all. The Greek historian Polybius wrote that the Romans "failed to reckon with the ability of Archimedes, nor did they foresee that in some circumstances the genius of one man is more effective than any number of hands."[4]

For two years, the products of Archimedes held back the Roman army. Marcellus persisted, and eventually he discovered a weakness in the walls of Syracuse. One evening in 212 B.C., the Greeks were busy celebrating a feast to the goddess Artemis. Roman troops found a carelessly guarded tower and climbed inside its walls. Soon after breaching the walls, the Romans occupied the entire city. The lives of most of the soldiers and citizens of Syracuse were spared. But as punishment for Syracuse, Marcellus ordered his soldiers to plunder the city.

The Death of Archimedes

Even though he fought against the Greeks, Marcellus admired and respected Archimedes. He recognized the genius of Archimedes' inventions. Marcellus also realized that Archimedes himself was not an enemy of Rome. When the Romans prepared to invade Syracuse, Marcellus gave instructions to his soldiers not to kill Archimedes. Archimedes was to be captured unharmed and brought directly to Marcellus.

But despite these orders, Archimedes was killed by a Roman soldier. Several different versions exist for how Archimedes died. Told by Plutarch, the most popular story says that a Roman soldier found Archimedes and demanded that the Greek accompany him. But as always, Archimedes was too interested in his mathematics. He refused to leave until he had found a solution for his problem. At this point, the soldier lost his temper and stabbed Archimedes with his sword.[5]

A similar account of this same story has the Roman soldier casting a shadow over a diagram Archimedes drew in the sand. Archimedes was concentrating on his problem so much that he was unaware of the events around him. His only concern was his mathematics, and he shouted, "Do not disturb my circles!" The soldier then killed Archimedes, and this statement has become famous as Archimedes' final words.[6]

Yet another story states that Archimedes did accompany the Roman soldier as ordered. In this version, Archimedes had his arms full of

In this depiction, Archimedes concentrates on a mathematical problem and is oblivious to the impending danger. Syracuse falls to Rome while Archimedes is struck dead by a Roman soldier.

scientific instruments, dials, angles, and small inventions. Mistaking these devices for gold or treasure, the Roman soldiers killed Archimedes and stole the instruments. No matter how Archimedes died, Marcellus regretted the actions of his soldiers. Marcellus had no reason to want Archimedes murdered.

The death of Archimedes effectively signaled the end of classical Greek science. This mark does not mean that the Greeks no longer researched or developed any new concepts. However, with the fall of Syracuse and the end of the Punic Wars, Rome was now the dominant power. Soon, Greek culture would be absorbed into the Roman Empire, and Greek science would become Roman science.

7

ARCHIMEDES THROUGH HISTORY

ARCHIMEDES IS OFTEN CONSIDERED THE greatest intellect of the ancient world. Some historians have even called him a thoroughly modern scientist. They believe Archimedes would be equally brilliant had he lived during the Renaissance, the nineteenth century, or even today. He is listed along with Isaac Newton and Karl Friedrich Gauss as the three greatest mathematicians of all time. Archimedes' importance to science and mathematics is difficult to overestimate.

Other mathematicians, scientists, historians, and writers have acknowledged the greatness of Archimedes throughout history. The French writer Voltaire wrote in the eighteenth century that Archimedes had a greater imagination than even the legendary Greek poet Homer.[1] The twentieth-century mathematician Alfred North Whitehead wrote: "No Roman lost his life because he was absorbed in the contemplation of a mathematical diagram."[2]

Archimedes' Contemporaries

The books that Archimedes wrote lasted far longer than his own life. His fame was known throughout the ancient world, and his books were copied and read by other scholars. Ancient Greek and Roman historians such as Polybius, Livy, and Plutarch continued to write about Archimedes and his discoveries.

Other ancient astronomers and mathematicians studied the books of Archimedes. Many would also write their own books, sometimes commenting or expanding on Archimedes' original work. In the fifth century A.D., the Greek mathematician Eutocius wrote commentaries about some of the books of Archimedes. These commentaries are some of the only sources that survive for Archimedes' work.

The Roman engineer Vitruvius wrote a detailed description of an Archimedean screw in his work *De Architectura* in the first century B.C. He did not mention Archimedes by name, and this simple machine is never mentioned by Archimedes in his writings. This screw has been used since ancient times, and it may have been named after Archimedes only because of his fame as an inventor. Later works like these helped keep ideas and tools like the Archimedean screw well known through the centuries.

Archimedes requested a specific favor of his friends and family upon his death. He wanted an inscription on his tomb of a cylinder circumscribing a sphere. This represented a proof he gave that the volume of the sphere is two-thirds that of the cylinder (2:3), and the surface area of the same sphere is also two-thirds that of the cylinder (2:3). Archimedes apparently regarded this proof as his greatest mathematical achievement.

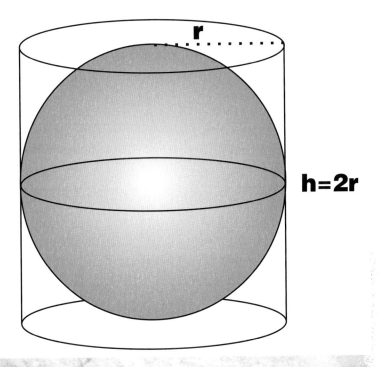

r

h=2r

Archimedes constructed a proof showing that the volume of a sphere is two-thirds that of a cylinder circumscribing it. The surface area of the sphere is also two-thirds that of the cylinder.

While a quaestor (a Roman official) of Sicily in 75 B.C., Cicero located this neglected tomb of Archimedes in Syracuse and ordered it restored. He recognized the grave by the symbol of the sphere and cylinder inscribed upon it. Cicero wrote: "So one of the most famous cities in the

Cicero and the magistrates come upon the tomb of Archimedes hidden behind thorny bushes. A stone sphere and cylinder sit above the tomb.

Greek world, and in former days a great center of learning as well, would have remained in total ignorance of the tomb of the most brilliant citizen it had ever produced, had a man from Arpinum not come and pointed it out."[3] However, the exact location of this site since then has been lost.

Early Translations

It is amazing that we know anything about Archimedes at all. Just as quickly as the manuscripts of Archimedes were copied, so were the originals often lost or destroyed. Most of the original work of Archimedes comes to us through Greek copies. Some we know through translations into other languages. These translations were used as textbooks to teach students and other scientists about these principles.

Many of these ancient Greek and Roman manuscripts traveled to the Middle East. The Arab caliphate was flourishing, and Arab scholars were eager to learn from the West. The ninth-century Arab astronomer and mathematician Thābit ibn Qurra translated many works of Archimedes into Arabic. By the year A.D. 1000, almost all Greek texts on medicine, science, and mathematics had been translated into Arabic.[4]

Just as many Greek and Roman manuscripts were translated into Arabic, in the twelfth century, these texts began to be translated from Arabic into Latin. Latin was widely regarded as the language of academics in Europe at that time. By making these manuscripts available in Latin, these ancient authors were reintroduced back to their native Europe a thousand years after they lived.

Another major translator was the Italian academic Gerard of Cremona, who lived during the twelfth century. Gerard converted many ancient texts from Arabic into Latin and reintroduced them to Europe. A Latin version of Archimedes' work *On Floating Bodies* was produced by the Flemish translator William of Moerbeke in the thirteenth century. This version was the primary record of this work of Archimedes until another source was discovered in the early twentieth century.[5]

Renaissance Discoveries

Books of ancient writers were both valuable and delicate objects. Paper and binding were rare and expensive, so books were constructed and written by hand. Not until the sixteenth century could books be printed more cheaply and easily. Once books could be printed, they spread to the universities across Europe. The knowledge these books held traveled widely and quickly, helping fuel the Renaissance.

Until the Renaissance, Archimedes was known mostly for his mechanical inventions. The stories and devices surrounding the ancient Greek scientist were of more interest than his theories. But in the late sixteenth century, translators began making Archimedes' mathematical works available. One of the major sources was the Italian translator Federigo Commandino. Commandino was responsible for the first complete mathematical texts of Archimedes in Latin.[6]

The sixteenth-century Italian scientist Galileo Galilei was greatly influenced by the works of Archimedes. Galileo admired Archimedes and was particularly interested in his work on hydrostatics. Inspired by the ancient scientist, Galileo built his own balance to measure the

Galileo Galilei (1564–1642), Italian astronomer and physicist.

buoyancy of objects in water. The first academic paper that Galileo wrote was about the principles of Archimedes.[7]

Archimedes influenced many of the great scientists and mathematicians of the Renaissance and later. The German astronomer Johannes Kepler used a method similar to that of Archimedes to calculate his own value of pi. The nineteenth-century French mathematician Marie-Sophie Germain was so moved as a child reading the story of Archimedes' murder that she decided to devote her life to mathematics.

The Archimedes Palimpsest

In 1906, a text was discovered by a modern historian from Denmark named Johan Ludwig Heiberg. Heiberg was an expert on ancient Greek history and especially about Archimedes and his work. He located this text in the library of a monastery in Constantinople in Turkey. This text was a palimpsest, or an ancient early version of a manuscript made from animal hide. The term *palimpsest* comes from the Greek term meaning "rescraping." Because paper was rare

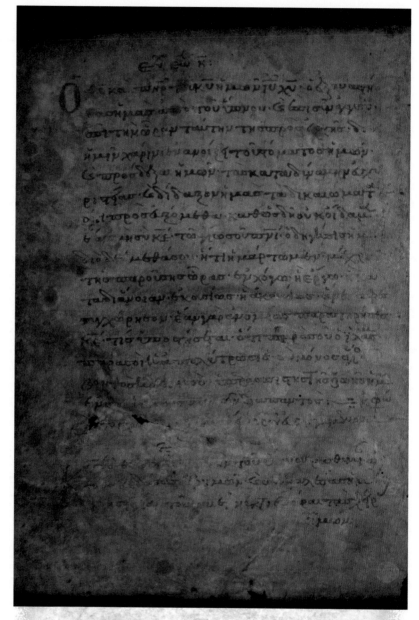

A close-up image of a page from the Archimedes palimpsest. The medieval prayers are the only writings visible.

An enhanced image of the same page. Now one can see the ancient text and diagrams underneath in white.

and valuable, an animal hide could be scraped clean and used again and again as a parchment for writing.

The original text of this palimpsest was already scraped off, and a thirteenth-century book of prayers was written on top of it. This palimpsest disappeared for almost a century after its discovery. It resurfaced in 1991, and in 1998 the volume was at an auction house in New York. This dirty, battered book was sold for $2,200,000 and then loaned to the Walters Art Museum in Baltimore, Maryland.

Because the palimpsest had been reused many times, it already had copies of older texts underneath. Beneath the newer text was text of ancient Greek that was not completely erased. Some of the older texts were known works of Archimedes. Sometime around A.D. 1000, several works of Archimedes were copied onto this palimpsest. Around the year 1200, a Christian monk erased the original texts and copied prayers in Greek onto the palimpsest.

The researchers at the museum teamed up with scientists to use modern technology to analyze the palimpsest. Some existing text could be read beneath the new prayers or in the margins of the pages. Other new text was also discovered under ultraviolet light. The researchers then took the palimpsest to the Stanford Linear Accelerator Center in California. Under highly focused X-rays, more text and diagrams were revealed that were not visible to the human eye.[8]

This palimpsest included copies of *On Floating Bodies, The Method,* and *Stomachion* before being reused as a prayer book. This copy of *The Method* is the only copy of this text by Archimedes known to exist. It is also the only copy of *On Floating Bodies* in the original Greek. Scientists were able to read not only the text but also the calculations and diagrams that were copied along with the text. Research on this palimpsest and its contents is still going on today.

8

ARCHIMEDES TODAY

THE WORK OF ARCHIMEDES SERVES AS the basis for many fields of science and mathematics. His books have been studied and expanded for more than two thousand years. Even today, the principles of Archimedes are still being researched and applied to new technology. Some historians call Archimedes the most important figure in the history of science.

Many of Archimedes' discoveries and inventions still find uses in our modern world. The Archimedean screw is still used in some rural parts of Egypt to pump water for irrigation. The principles of statics and hydrostatics are still taught to modern-day students using the same methods that

Archimedes used. His mathematical texts continue to be studied by students and mathematicians.

The Archimedes spiral has many uses in engineering applications. Two Archimedes spirals interlaced together form a mechanism to convert circular motion into linear motion. This method is used in a device called a scroll compressor, which is used to compress liquids and gases. The uniform design of an Archimedes spiral is also good for parts within mechanical clocks, phonographs, or any device that requires regular circular motion.

Archimedes' work on the method of exhaustion was an early exploration of the ideas of modern calculus. Calculus was developed by Isaac Newton and Gottfried Wilhelm Leibniz in the seventeenth century. Today, calculus is part of almost every field of science and engineering. Its ability to describe the properties of objects in motion makes it critical to applications from economic analysis to auto racing to building spacecraft.

The many inventions and discoveries of Archimedes still continue to fascinate us. Many modern scientists and engineers have tried to construct devices originally described by Archimedes. Some want to prove the physics behind the device, and some want to test the historical accuracy of these stories. Historians still debate which tales are true and which are legends.

In 1973, a Greek engineer named Ioannis Sakkas demonstrated Archimedes' mirrored superweapon (or "death ray"). He used only tools and knowledge that the ancient Greeks would have had. Sakkas used seventy reflective copper lenses to focus the rays of the sun on a wooden ship. The ship caught fire within three minutes, proving that Archimedes' weapon was possible.[1] Sakkas continues to test the inventions of Archimedes.

In 2005, a mechanical engineer named David Wallace also tried to test the idea of Archimedes' mirror. He and his students at the Massachusetts Institute of Technology (MIT)

MIT students set up and cover the 127 mirrors for the death ray experiment in 2005.

The ship ignites ten minutes after the mirrors are focused.

95

The MIT group redid the death ray experiment on the Discovery Channel's *Mythbusters*. This time they used three hundred mirrors arranged in four tiers.

built a replica of a Roman ship and used 127 mirrored tiles to focus the light of the sun. After about ten minutes, the ship burst into flames.[2] However, both Sakkas's and Wallace's work shows this invention would have been difficult to use if the enemy ships were moving.

The Discovery Channel show *MythBusters* has also attempted to test the inventions of

Archimedes in several episodes. Other shows such as BBC's *Secrets of the Ancients* and Discovery Channel's *Superweapons of the Ancient World* have done the same. Devices such as Archimedes' mirrored weapon and his steam cannon have been built, each with some successes and failures.[3] Our curiosity surrounding Archimedes and his inventions seem endless.

The team had a harder time igniting the thirty-foot fishing boat than they did igniting the Roman ship replica, but they ultimately succeeded. Both experiments showed that although Archimedes' death ray was plausible, it would not have been a practical form of defense.

Archimedes has developed into not only a respected historical figure but also part of our collective culture. Craters on the moon and academic awards are named after him. His face appears on postage stamps, coins, and in paintings and sculpture. Archimedes' name is seen in locations around the world, far from Rome or Greece. Even today, the term *Eureka!* is still used to represent a sudden discovery or revelation.

ACTIVITIES

Activity 1

Using a Lever

Archimedes was one of the first scientists to investigate how a lever worked. He reduced the physics to a mathematical principle that is still used today. Because there are no restrictions on the mathematics, the same principle is valid for ounces as well as tons.

Materials needed:
- a flat 12-inch ruler
- a round cardboard tube
- several different coins (pennies, nickels, dimes, quarters)
- tape

Procedure:

Tape the cardboard tube down on the surface of a desk or table, so that it cannot move.

Balance the ruler on the tube at the 6-inch mark. This is the balance point for the unloaded lever at equilibrium. The 6-inch mark will be used to mark the fulcrum.

A simple playground seesaw functions on the same principle as a lever.

Place two of the same coins on either end of the ruler and try to balance the lever. Note that because the coins' masses are equal, the lever will only balance if the coins are the same distance from the fulcrum.

Try to balance different coins on either end of the ruler. A heavier mass can be balanced by a lighter mass if the lighter mass is further from the fulcrum.

Advanced:

Using the law of the lever as $m_1d_1 = m_2d_2$, calculate the mass of a different coin, or the mass of an unknown object. (Hint: A U.S. nickel has a mass of 5 grams.)

Activity 2

Finding the Center of Gravity

Archimedes calculated the centers of gravity of many different shapes. Most of these were regular geometrical shapes, so the centers of gravity could be found mathematically. However, for irregularly shaped objects the center of gravity can also be determined experimentally.

Materials:

◈ a piece of cardboard or heavy paper
◈ a piece of string

❖ a small weight, like a screw or a washer
❖ a paper clip
❖ a pencil or marker
❖ scissors

Procedure:

On the cardboard, draw a shape with a pencil and cut it out with the scissors. Try to avoid regular geometrical shapes like circles, squares, or triangles.

Tie the small weight to one end of the string. Loop the other end through the paper clip.

Punch a small hold on the edge of the cardboard shape and thread it through the paper clip. The cardboard shape should be able to hang freely from the paper clip.

Hold the paper clip, letting the cardboard shape and the string hang straight down. Note where the line of the string falls on the cardboard, and mark this line with a pencil.

Repeat Steps 3 and 4 using a different location on the cardboard shape. (These steps may be repeated as many times as necessary.)

The center of gravity of an object will always lie on a line directly beneath its point of suspension. Where the lines cross on this cardboard shape will be its center of gravity.

Activity 3

Demonstrating Buoyancy

Archimedes' principle states that an object in water will be supported by a force equal to the weight of the water displaced by that object. This is the principle of buoyancy, and it explains why cargo ships made of steel and weighing thousands of tons can float on the ocean.

Materials:

- ◈ three aluminum pie pans
- ◈ at least one hundred pennies, washers, or other small weights
- ◈ a sink or tub filled with water

Procedure:

Take one pie pan and crush it into a small, tight ball. Fold a second pie pan in half to form a small boat, and crimp the edges to make it water-tight. Leave the third pie pan whole.

Place the pie pans on the water, all at once if space allows or one at a time. All three pie pans have identical weights but different shapes. Their masses are the same, but each displaces a different volume of water.

Begin loading the pie pans with pennies. How many pennies can they hold before they sink? Which shape holds the most pennies?

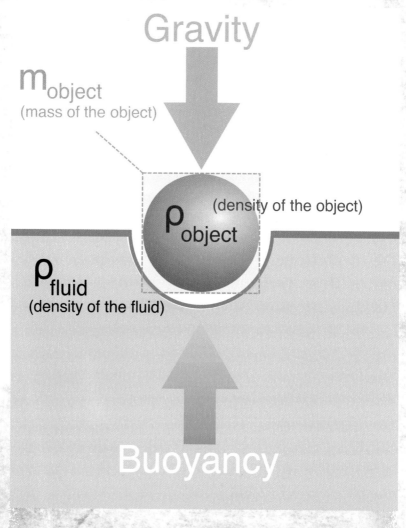

This diagram illustrates Archimedes' principle of buoyancy.

The crushed pie pan should sink because it does not displace enough water to offset its own weight. The other two pie pans can support themselves plus much heavier weights because their shapes displace a larger volume of water.

CHRONOLOGY

c. 730 B.C.—The city of Syracuse is founded.

306 B.C.—King Ptolemy I becomes king of Egypt. Ptolemy I founds Mouseion and library in Alexandria.

287 B.C.—Archimedes is born, probably in Syracuse.

285–286 B.C.—King Ptolemy II rules Egypt. Attracts scholars and intellectuals to Alexandria. Expands collection of papyrus scrolls in library.

278 B.C.—Pyrrhus becomes king of the island of Sicily.

275 B.C.—Hiero II gains control of Syracuse, later to become king.

c. 250 B.C.—Archimedes studies in Alexandria.

218 B.C.—The Second Punic War begins.

215 B.C.—Hiero II dies of natural causes.

212 B.C.—Archimedes is murdered by a Roman soldier.

201 B.C.—The Second Punic War ends.

106 B.C.—Roman statesman and philosopher Cicero is born.

75 B.C.—Cicero discovers Archimedes' neglected tomb.

first century B.C.—Roman writer and engineer Vitruvius describes Archimedes' test of Hiero's gold crown.

A.D. c. 46—Roman biographer and historian Plutarch is born.

second century—Roman writer Lucius describes Archimedes' mirror weapon.

fifth century—Greek mathematician Eutocius writes commentaries on Archimedes' work.

ninth century—Arab mathematician Thābit ibn Qurra translates Archimedes' works into Arabic.

twelfth century—Gerard of Cremona translates Archimedes' works into Latin.

c. 1229—An unknown Christian monk erases the original texts of the Archimedes Palimpsest.

1543—Copernicus publishes his heliocentric model of the universe.

seventeenth century—Newton and Leibniz both independently develop calculus.

1906—Heiberg discovers the Archimedes Palimpsest in Constantinople.

1974—Sakkas builds and tests a prototype of Archimedes' mirror weapon.

1998—The Archimedes Palimpsest is sold at auction for 2 million dollars; it is later loaned to the Walters Art Museum for analysis.

1999—*The Method* is discovered in the Archimedes Palimpsest, the only copy known to exist.

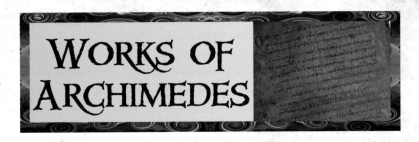

WORKS OF ARCHIMEDES

On the Equilibrium of Planes (two volumes)

These books are probably the most significant of Archimedes' works. They detail the basic principles and foundation of mechanics. More than the two volumes may have been written by Archimedes, but only these two books survive.

Quadrature of the Parabola

This book is a work of purely mathematical problems involving the parabola. Archimedes includes his method of exhaustion in these proofs.

On the Sphere and Cylinder (two volumes)

These books are works of mathematical theory of three-dimensional objects. Here Archimedes proves the ratio of the volumes of a cylinder to an inscribed sphere, a proof he wanted engraved on his tomb.

On Spirals

This book is a study of plane geometry. Specifically, it is an investigation of the properties of what is known today as the Archimedes spiral.

On Conoids and Spheroids

This book is a study of solid geometry. Archimedes deals with calculating the solid volumes of spheres, cones, and cylinders.

Another similar book is referred to by Pappus, but this work has never been found.

On Floating Bodies (two volumes)

These are books about the principles of hydrostatics. Archimedes includes complicated problems of buoyancy, displacement, and the Archimedes principle.

Measurement of the Circle

This is another book of pure mathematics, mostly concerned with aspects of the circle. In this book, Archimedes calculates the value of pi using his method of exhaustion.

The Sand-Reckoner (Psammites, Arenarius)

This is one of Archimedes' books on pure mathematics. He demonstrates an understanding of the arithmetic of large numbers far greater than that of any other ancient mathematician.

Stomachion

This is a geometrical puzzle of fourteen pieces that fit together to form a square. Archimedes tried to calculate the number of different solutions to this puzzle.

The Method of Mechanical Theorems (or The Method)

This was one of the lost books of Archimedes that was discovered in 1906 by historian Johan Ludwig Heiberg in a library in Constantinople. It provides an insight as to how Archimedes thought out solutions to his theories.

On Sphere-Making (lost)

This book is one that we know Archimedes wrote, but it has never been found. It describes the construction of an astronomical tool known today as a planetarium.

On Balances (lost)

This is another book that Archimedes wrote, but it has never been found. It is a book of the mathematics around arithmetic, geometry, and equilibrium.

Naming of Numbers (lost)

The exact title of this book is not known, but its existence is referred to in another book by Archimedes. It expanded on the naming system for very large numbers used in *The Sand-Reckoner*.

Catoptrica (lost)

This book deals with the theory of optics and mirrors. Its existence is referred to by the ancient Greek mathematician Theon of Alexandria. However, a copy of this work has never been found.

Book of Lemmas

This is a collection of various small problems and mathematical theorems. The original has been lost, but an Arabic translation survives.

The Cattle Problem

This is a riddle that was credited to Archimedes, although many doubt he actually wrote it. The riddle describes the number of differently colored bulls and cows in a field, and the solution involves very large numbers.

Many other works have been credited to Archimedes by Arabic translators. However, whether or not Archimedes actually wrote these books is not known for certain. Some of these books could be ideas originally from Archimedes but written by someone else.

CHAPTER NOTES

Chapter 1. Life in Syracuse

1. George Willis Botsford and Charles Alexander Robinson, Jr., *Hellenic History,* 4th ed. (New York: Macmillan Company, 1956), p. 281.

2. Ibid., pp. 380–381.

3. Vivian Shaw Groza, *A Survey of Mathematics* (New York: Holt, Rinehart and Winston, 1968), pp.100–101.

4. L. Sprague de Camp, *The Ancient Engineers: Technology and Invention From the Earliest Times to the Renaissance* (New York: Barnes and Noble Books, 1993), p. 162.

5. Plutarch, *The Lives of the Noble Grecians and Romans,* trans. John Dryden (New York: Random House, 1932), p. 378.

6. Reviel Netz and William Noel, *The Archimedes Codex: How a Medieval Prayer Book Is Revealing the True Genius of Antiquity's Greatest Scientist* (Philadelphia: Da Capo Press, 2007), p. 15.

Chapter 2. Archimedes as Mathematician

1. L. Sprague de Camp, *The Ancient Engineers: Technology and Invention From the Earliest Times to the Renaissance* (New York: Barnes & Noble Books, 1993), p. 149.

2. Carl B. Boyer, *A History of Mathematics* (New York: John Wiley & Sons, 1968), p. 178.

3. Thomas L. Heath, *The Works of Archimedes* (Cambridge, U.K.: Cambridge University Press, 1897), p. 154.

4. E. T. Bell, *Men of Mathematics* (New York: Simon & Schuster, 1986), p. 30.

5. Petr Beckmann, *A History of Pi* (New York: St. Martin's Press, 1971), p. 64.

6. Heath, p. 92.

7. Ibid., p. 222.

8. James R. Newman, *The World of Mathematics* (New York: Simon & Schuster, 1956), vol. 1, p. 426.

9. Reviel Netz and William Noel, *The Archimedes Codex: How a Medieval Prayer Book Is Revealing the True Genius of Antiquity's Greatest Scientist* (Philadelphia: Da Capo Press, 2007), p. 55.

Chapter 3. Hiero's Gold Crown

1. Arnold Reymond, *History of the Sciences in Greco-Roman Antiquity,* trans. Ruth Gheury de Bray (New York: Bibio & Tannen, 1963), p. 75.

2. James R. Newman, *The World of Mathematics* (New York: Simon & Schuster, 1956), vol. 1, p. 186.

3. Carl B. Boyer, *A History of Mathematics* (New York: John Wiley & Sons, 1968), p. 137.

4. Clifford A. Pickover, *Archimedes to Hawking: Laws of Science and the Great Minds Behind Them* (New York: Oxford University Press, 2008), p. 41.

5. Boyer, p. 137.

Chapter 4. On the Equilibrium of Planes

1. Plutarch, *The Lives of the Noble Grecians and Romans,* trans. John Dryden (New York: Random House, 1932), p. 376.

2. Carl B. Boyer, *A History of Mathematics* (New York: John Wiley & Sons, 1968), p. 136.

3. David C. Lindberg, *The Beginnings of Western Science: The European Scientific Tradition in Philosophical, Religious, and Institutional Context, 600* B.C. *to* A.D.

1450 (Chicago: University of Chicago Press, 1992), pp. 109–110.

4. Vivian Shaw Groza, *A Survey of Mathematics: Elementary Concepts and Their Historical Development* (New York: Holt, Rinehart & Winston, 1968), p. 101.

5. Reviel Netz and William Noel, *The Archimedes Codex: How a Medieval Prayer Book Is Revealing the True Genius of Antiquity's Greatest Scientist* (Philadelphia: Da Capo Press, 2007), p. 142.

6. Netz and Noel, p. 53.

Chapter 5. Other Inventions

1. L. Sprague de Camp, *The Ancient Engineers: Technology and Invention From the Earliest Times to the Renaissance* (New York: Barnes & Noble Books, 1993), p. 159.

2. "Archimedes of Syracuse," *Thessaloniki Science Center and Technology Museum*, 2001, <http://www.tmth.edu.gr/en/aet/1/13.html> (May 28, 2008).

3. Plutarch, *The Lives of the Noble Grecians and Romans*, trans. John Dryden (New York: Random House, 1932), pp. 376–377.

4. M. I. Finley, *Ancient Sicily* (Totowa, N.J.: Rowman & Littlefield, 1979), p. 120.

5. Arnold Reymond, *History of the Sciences in Greco-Roman Antiquity*, trans. Ruth Gheury de Bray (New York: Bibio & Tannen, 1963), p. 71.

6. Paul Bentley Kern, *Ancient Siege Warfare* (Bloomington, Ind.: Indianapolis University Press, 1999), p. 263.

Chapter 6. The Sack of Syracuse

1. T. A. Dorey and D. R. Dudley, *Rome Against Carthage: A History of the Punic Wars* (Garden City, N.Y.: Doubleday & Company, 1972), p. 122.

2. Ibid., p. 123.

3. Plutarch, *The Lives of the Noble Grecians and Romans,* trans. John Dryden (New York: Random House, 1932), p. 378.

4. M. I. Finley, *Ancient Sicily* (Totowa, N.J.: Rowman & Littlefield, 1979), p. 118.

5. Plutarch, p. 380.

6. E. T. Bell, *Men of Mathematics* (New York: Simon & Schuster, 1986), p. 34.

Chapter 7. Archimedes Through History

1. Lloyd Motz and Jefferson Hane Weaver, *The Story of Mathematics* (New York: Plenum Press, 1993), p. 22.

2. Herbert Westren Turnbull, "The Great Mathematicians," in *The World of Mathematics,* by James R. Newman (New York: Simon & Schuster, 1956), vol. 1, p. 104.

3. Marcus Tulius Cicero, *On the Good Life,* trans. Michael Grant (New York: Penguin Books, 1971), pp. 86–87.

4. David C. Lindberg, *The Beginnings of Western Science: The European Scientific Tradition in Philosophical, Religious, and Institutional Context, 600 B.C. to A.D. 1450* (Chicago: University of Chicago Press, 1992), p. 170.

5. Thomas L. Heath, *A Manual of Greek Mathematics* (New York: Dover Publications, 1963), p. 283.

6. Marie Boas, *The Scientific Renaissance: 1450–1630* (New York: Harper & Row, 1962), p. 226.

7. James Reston, Jr., *Galileo: A Life* (New York: HarperCollins, 1994), p. 19.

8. Reviel Netz and William Noel, *The Archimedes Codex: How a Medieval Prayer Book Is Revealing the*

True Genius of Antiquity's Greatest Scientist (Philadelphia: Da Capo Press, 2007), p. 273.

Chapter 8. Archimedes Today

1. "Archimedes of Syracuse," *Thessaloniki Science Center and Technology Museum*, 2001, <http://www.tmth.edu.gr/en/aet/1/13.html> (May 28, 2008).

2. Clifford A. Pickover, *Archimedes to Hawking: Laws of Science and the Great Minds Behind Them* (New York: Oxford University Press, 2008), pp. 44–45.

3. "*MythBusters*: Episode Guide," *Discovery Channel*, 2009, <http://dsc.discovery.com/fansites/mythbusters/episode/episode-tab-03.html> (May 26, 2008).

GLOSSARY

Archimedean screw—A screw pump used to manually transfer water from a lower to a higher level.

Archimedes principle—The buoyant force of an object in water equals the weight of the water displaced by the object.

Artemis—In Greek mythology, the goddess of nature and fertility (known as Diana in Roman mythology).

Briareus—A giant from Greek mythology with fifty heads and one hundred arms.

buoyancy—The upward force of the surrounding water on a submerged object.

caliphate—A unified Islamic government ruled by a caliph, or head of state.

center of gravity—The point on an object at which the total mass of the object seems to balance.

circumference—The total length along the outside of a circle.

city-state—An independent, self-governing city that does not belong to any nation.

compound pulley—A combination of fixed and moving pulleys acting together.

consul—The highest elected political office of the Roman Republic.

cylinder—A solid figure with two equal parallel circular bases and straight sides.

density—The ratio of mass per unit volume.

diameter—A straight line that passes from one side of a circle to the other through the circle's center point.

displacement—A volume of water displaced, or "pushed aside," by a submerged object.

equilibrium—The state of a system in balance where all opposing forces result in no net change.

force—The cause that puts an object at rest into motion.

fulcrum—The fixed point about which a lever turns.

geometry—The branch of mathematics that deals with the properties and relations of points, lines, shapes, and solids.

heliocentric model—A model of the solar system that has the sun at the center orbited by the earth and the other planets.

hydrostatics—The branch of science related to the study of pressure and equilibrium in liquids.

irrational number—A number that cannot be written as a repeating or finite decimal (for example, = 3.1415926...).

kinetics—The branch of mechanics that studies forces acting on an object in motion.

lever—A simple machine that consists of a rigid bar that pivots around a fixed point.

Magna Graecia—An area of Greek colonies at the southern tip of Italy and the island of Sicily.

mechanical advantage—The property of a machine to multiply the force put into it to produce a larger force.

mechanics—The field of physics that deals with forces acting on an object. It includes statics and kinetics.

myriad—The ancient Greek value of ten thousand (denoted as *M*).

numeral—A written symbol referring to a number value.

palimpsest—A manuscript made from an animal hide that has been reused by scraping off the original text.

papyrus—Writing material made from the papyrus plant, a tall reed that grows in Egypt.

perimeter—The total length along the outer boundary of a figure.

pi—The ratio of the circumference of a circle to its diameter (π).

planetarium—A mechanical model of the night sky that demonstrates the respective and proportional motion of stars and planets as seen from the earth.

polygon—A two-dimensional shape made with three or more sides of the same length.

pulley—A grooved wheel that a rope or cord can pass over.

quaestor—An elected office of the Roman Republic that supervised the treasury and financial matters of state.

radius—A straight line from the center to the circumference of a circle or sphere.

Renaissance—The transitional period from about the fourteenth century to the seventeenth century, during which the ancient texts were rediscovered and reintroduced to Europe (taken from the French word for "rebirth").

siege—A military operation in which a fortified place is surrounded by an attacking force.

simple machines—The basic machines of physics: lever, wheel, pulley, inclined plane, screw, and wedge.

statics—The branch of mechanics that studies forces acting on an object at equilibrium.

volume—The three-dimensional amount of space occupied by an object.

FURTHER READING

Books

Hasan, Heather. *Archimedes: The Father of Mathematics.* New York: Rosen Publishing, 2006.

Herweck, Don. *Mechanical Engineering.* Mankato, Minn.: Compass Point Books, 2008.

Plummer, Todd. *I've Discovered Force!* Tarrytown, N.Y.: Marshall Cavendish, 2009.

Sawa, Maureen. *The Library Book: The Story of Libraries from Camels to Computers.* Toronto: Tundra Books, 2006.

Staeger, Rob. *Ancient Mathematicians.* Greensboro, N.C.: Morgan Reynolds, 2007.

Zannos, Susan. *The Life and Times of Archimedes.* Hockessin, Del.: Mitchell Lane Publishers, 2005.

INTERNET ADDRESSES

Archimedes' Laboratory
http://www.archimedes-lab.org

The Archimedes Palimpsest
http://www.archimedespalimpsest.org

Chris Rorres: Archimedes
www.cs..edu/~crorres/Archimedes/contents.html

Exploratorium: Ancient Writings Revealed!
http://www.exploratorium.edu/archimedes

INDEX